Our Clothes

Jeni Wilson and Sue Davis

Contents

Why We Put On Clothes

We **like** to put on clothes.

We put on warm clothes
when it is cold and wet.

We put on
other kinds of clothes
when it is very hot.

There are clothes that stop us
from getting hurt.

Clothes can help us
to look good and feel good.

All Kinds of Clothes

There are many kinds of clothes.

We have clothes
to sleep in.

We have clothes
to swim in.

Some children
have clothes like this
for school.

7

Clothes to Keep Us Safe

Shoes and boots help to stop our feet from getting hurt.

We put gloves on, to keep our hands warm.

We put hats and shirts on,
to keep the sun off our skin.

Work Clothes

Some clothes
are just for work.
People put on these clothes
to keep themselves safe.

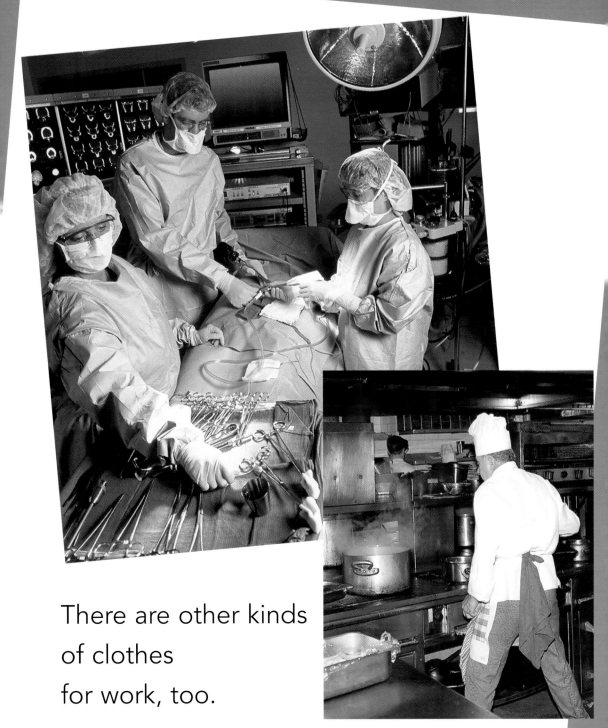

There are other kinds
of clothes
for work, too.

Clothes for Fun and Sports

Some people who play sports
put on pads and helmets.

Sometimes people
who are just having fun
put on pads
and helmets, too.

People on sports teams
have clothes that all look the same.
Then everyone knows who belongs
to each team.

There are all kinds of clothes
for playing sports.

Clothes for Special Times

The stage

People in plays dress up.
They try to look like someone
or something else.

The circus

Clowns put on
funny clothes
to make us laugh.

Going out

Sometimes we put on our best clothes when we are going out.

These children are going to a friend's birthday party.

Weddings

These people have dressed up for a wedding.

The clothes for a wedding are very special.

Festivals

These children have dressed up, too.
Lots of people are watching them.

How to Make a Party Hat

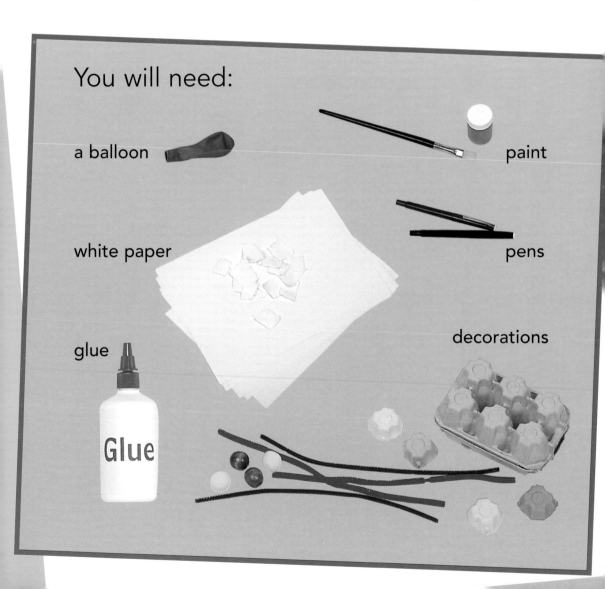

You will need:

a balloon   paint

white paper   pens

glue   decorations

1. Blow up the balloon.

2. Glue small bits
   of white paper
   all over the top
   of the balloon.

3. Let the glue dry.

4. Glue more bits of paper
   onto the balloon.

5. Let the glue dry
   until the paper is hard.

6. Pop the balloon.

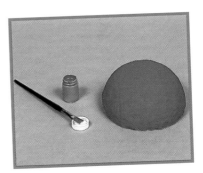

7. Paint your hat.

8. Put other things
   on your hat
   to make it look good.

What Clothes Are Made From

wool

silk

cotton

leather

Many clothes are made from things around us.

DID YOU KNOW?

New kinds of sports clothes can help people to run faster.

These clothes are made from other things.

Clothes Have Changed

DID YOU KNOW?

Long ago, people's clothes were made from animal skins, leaves and grass.

Clothes have not always
looked like they do today.

Questions

1. What can help people to run faster?

2. What did people make their clothes from, long ago?

Glossary

change	*not the same as it was*
dress	*to put on clothes*
helmet	*a hard, strong hat*